Active Books for ADHD

Outside the box books for kids and adults with ADHD

Written by Melissa Gijsbers

©2025 Melissa Gijsbers
melissagijsbers.com

Finish This Book Press

Written by Melissa Gijsbers

Cover Design using elements from Canva

ISBN: 978-0-6459968-9-0

All rights reserved. Apart from any permitted use under the Copyright Act, no part of this book may be reproduced, copied, scanned, stored in a retrieval system, recorded or transmitted in any form or by any means, without the prior permission of the publisher.

Dedication

For all those with ADHD who find it hard to sit still and read, may this book inspire a new way of thinking about reading.

Table of Contents

Dedication iii

Table of Contents iv

Introduction 1

Chapter 1 – What are 'Active' books? 3

Chapter 2 – Lift-the-flap and Touch and Feel books 5

Chapter 3 – Choose Your Own Adventure Books 7

Chapter 4 – Audiobooks 9

Chapter 5 – Cookbooks 11

Chapter 6 – Short Stories 13

Chapter 7 – Joke Books 16

Chapter 8 – Non-Fiction and Trivia Books 18

Chapter 9 – Crosswords, Word Searches & Puzzle Books 21

Chapter 10 – Atlas and Maps 23

Conclusion 25

About the Author 26

Books by Melissa 28

Introduction

Often, when you have ADHD, the idea of sitting still & reading feels too hard. Staying still when you need to move can feel like torture. The book may feel too long. You may not remember what happened last time you read so you must re-read sections before you can move on, and so much more.

It's not that we don't want to read a book. Reading can be an enjoyable activity. Stories often feature characters with ADHD, whether they realise it or not, and can provide a wonderful escape into another world.

Looking back over my own life, I am autistic and ADHD, I have found what I call 'active' books. These are books that invite you to do more than sit and read a story. They are still reading and can be enjoyable.

If you are a parent of a child or teen with ADHD, or have ADHD yourself, give some of these 'active' books a try and see what happens.

Chapter 1 – What are 'Active' books?

Active books are a term that I came up with when I was trying to give some suggestions to a mum who asked me for some tips on encouraging her ADHD son to read.

Most novels are written in a way where you need to sit still and read for a length of time.

Active books are ones that encourage you to do something as you read. One obvious example is a cookbook. You can sit and read it from cover to cover, and I have done that once or twice, though they are designed for you to read a recipe and then cook the food.

For many people, they don't realise that they are reading as they are cooking. The vocabulary is often rich with cooking terms and can engage readers who are interested in cooking. I will talk more about these later.

Active books come in many different types and can appeal to different readers of different ages.

As a parent who is autistic and ADHD, I often found these helped engage me and connect with my kids as they are often books we can enjoy together.

In the following chapters, I will share with you some different types of what I call 'active' books, some may have some recommendations, and I will highlight the benefits of different types of books.

Not all books will appeal to everyone, so try different books and see what works for you.

Remember that reading doesn't have to be limited to only reading fiction. Reading non-fiction is also reading.

Chapter 2 – Lift-the-flap and Touch and Feel books

If you are the parent of a toddler, you may find it hard for them to sit still and listen to a story. I found this with my older child. He was not one to sit still if there was something else for him to do.

It wasn't until we were given some touch & feel books that he started to sit still and engage with books as the touch and feel element gave him something to do.

After those, we moved on to lift the flap books, which he also enjoyed.

The touch and feel element to the books, as well as lifting the flaps gives the child something to do while you are reading the story. They can experience different textures and lift the flap to reveal a new element of the story.

They are able to engage in the story as something to do rather than having to sit still and listen quietly, waiting to turn the page.

There are many of these books on the market from books like *That's Not My...* series of touch and feel books, to lift the flap books like *Spot* by Eric Hill. There are also many non-fiction lift the flap books so you can find books based on the child's interests.

Chapter 3 – Choose Your Own Adventure Books

I grew up on the original *Choose Your Own Adventure Books* during the 1980s and 1990s. There were so many things to love about them. There were so many different types of stories, and you could, as the series said, choose your own adventure.

Looking back, I realise how much this appealed to my ADHD brain. The stories were not predictable as you could change the ending based on your choices. If you change your mind, you can either go back to your last option, if you remember where it was, or simply start again for a different result.

These books were amazing for a dopamine hit, and some of the adventures were shorter than others. They also looked like novels, so parents and teachers were happy to count them towards reading programs. I have also realised that they are quite tricky as if you go through them more than once, you may actually be reading more than expected.

The way the books are designed are also great for those with short attention spans, which can be common for those of us with ADHD, and we don't have to retain a lot of information about what comes before, which can also be a challenge for some.

I include these books in the category of 'active' books as the act of making decisions as well as going backwards and forward through the options adds an element of activity into the book.

These days, there are many different types of choose your own adventure books, so it's well worth talking with your local librarian or bookseller about books that are coming out now. You can also find copies of the original series in libraries and op shops.

Chapter 4 – Audiobooks

So many people think audiobooks are not reading, however I disagree. There are so many ways audiobooks are a benefit to those with ADHD.

When I was young, we used to listen to books on cassette and read along with the book. There was a 'ding' to turn the page. While those types of books may no longer exist, you can get an audiobook and follow along with the print or ebook if you wanting to follow the words.

Playing audiobooks while doing other things that may be considered 'boring' like doing the housework or driving in the car, can help some with ADHD get things done. If you have an ADHD child who struggles to tidy their room, for example, try playing an audiobook while they do the task and see what happens. My children used to go to sleep listening to audiobooks.

With an audiobook, you may not be looking at the words, but you are still experiencing the story.

There are many ways you can listen to audiobooks. You can go old school and get them on CD, listen via apps such as Borrow Box and Libby that you can get access to through your local library, as well as pay for subscriptions such as Audible.

Chapter 5 – Cookbooks

When you think of reading, I can almost guarantee that you won't immediately think of reading a cookbook. I know I don't. I can think of only one cookbook that I have read cover to cover, like you would a novel.

That said, there is a lot of reading involved when choosing recipes in a cookbook, and this can be engaging for many with ADHD.

If cooking is not your think, feel free to skip this section.

Cookbooks invite the reader to do something. You can read them in small bursts of time as you are looking for something to cook. There are new words to discover with new ingredients and methods. Added to that the activity of cooking once you have chosen a recipe.

For younger readers, there are cookbooks aimed at children and teenagers with simpler cooking methods. Younger readers may need supervision in the kitchen when they are learning to use knives and cook on stoves and in ovens.

Cooking is a valuable skill for everyone, and cookbooks can be wonderful things to read if cooking is a special interest. Cooking is not something I particularly enjoy, but I do remember spending hours reading the *Women's Weekly Birthday Cake Book* in the lead up to my birthday to decide what I wanted and going through everything needed to create the birthday cake of my dreams.

It's worth noting that, for many with ADHD, cooking can also be a challenge if there are too many steps, so it can be worth starting with some simple recipes and going from there.

Chapter 6 – Short Stories

Anthologies and collections of short stories may not be obvious as an active book, but they can appeal to those with ADHD.

An anthology is a collection of works by multiple authors and a collection is by a single author. Other than that, there isn't much difference between they two. They are books that contain a number of different short stories.

The beauty of short stories is that you can pick up a book and put it down after reading one or two stories, and you don't have to remember what happened last time you read. For younger writers, these books look like novels, so they may not have the same feeling of 'missing out' when their peers are reading novels.

Many authors have either published a short story collection of their own or contributed to anthologies, including some well-known authors. Their short stories may not be as well-known as some of their longer works, however they are still enjoyable.

I include these in the category of 'active' books as these are books that are easy to pick up and put down. The reader doesn't have to commit to sitting and reading longer stories, and they also don't have to worry about forgetting the story before moving on.

As well as short story collections, poetry collections also fit in this category. When I was growing up, I loved reading the *Far Out, Brussell Sprout* and *Alright, Vegemite* books of silly poems for kids. As an adult, there have been a few poetry collections that I have really enjoyed.

Short story and poetry collections can also make fantastic bedtime stories for parents and children with ADHD as you can be reading a book at bedtime, but neither of you has to remember what happened in the previous chapter!

Chapter 7 – Joke Books

If there is one type of book that is designed to drive parents wild, it is joke books, however these are wonderful books to get kids reading.

There are many different joke books for different ages and stages, and kids will have fun reading jokes for parents and others to answer.

They may not have a story, however many do have a wide vocabulary as well as show different ways to use words in order for the jokes to make sense, so are a wonderful way to increase a child's vocabulary.

As an adult, these can also be fun to read and share with your kids as well as your social group. They can be a great way to break the ice, if that is an issue.

Joke books are another type of book you can pick up and put down as the mood strikes as well as one that can inspire social interactions.

Chapter 8 – Non-Fiction and Trivia Books

When my kids were small, we had a lot of non-fiction books about various things my kids were interested in. At various times this included pirates, AFL Football, reptiles, animals, trains, space, and many other topics.

These were the sorts of books that the kids could pick up, read a few pages, then put down. The vocabulary was varied as they would contain technical terms, as well as being on topics my children were interested in.

With trivia books, we found some based on the topics of interest as well as books that contained random facts. Books like the *Guinness World Records* fall into this category.

These books had my kids hooked and there were times when they would sit reading them for hours as it was a topic that was interesting to them. At other times, they would browse a few pages, then leave the book for a while before looking up something else.

Many of these books can also inspire activities. If they are reading a non-fiction book about architecture, for example, it may inspire them to read a book about building things, then inspire them to make something.

Random bits of trivia can always come in handy and you never know what sort of rabbit hole they may inspire.

Even as an adult, I enjoy reading these sorts of non-fiction and fact books. I like books I can dip in and out of, and I enjoy learning random pieces of information.

Another sort of book that my kids enjoyed were books like *The Numbers Game* by Adam

Spencer. This book is about maths and numbers, something my son enjoyed, and had facts as well as number problems for him to solve.

Chapter 9 – Crosswords, Word Searches & Puzzle Books

When talking about books and reading, this may seem like an odd section to include, however there is a surprising amount of reading involved in solving a crossword puzzle.

Crosswords can also help with practicing handwriting, however that is a topic for another book.

There are crosswords, word searches and other word puzzle books aimed at every age and stage, and there are ones on specific topics if you are looking for resources to support a hyperfocus or hobby.

These books are also great to have on hand if you are looking for a screen free activity when out and about as smaller ones can easily fit in a bag, ready to be brought out at a café, waiting room, or anywhere you need to sit still for a while. The act of filling out the crossword or doing the word search can serve as a stim (a self-stimulatory behaviour).

Another benefit of a crossword is that it may inspire a new interest by finding a clue or word particularly interesting so the reader will want to find out more about that topic.

Chapter 10 – Atlas and Maps

When my kids were small, their Opa (grandfather) was given an atlas for Christmas. They wanted to know what it was, and our explanation was 'Google maps in a book!'

This led to many hours poring over the atlas learning about different place names and countries.

The atlas had facts about countries as well as detailed maps. This one was aimed at adults rather than being one for children, but it was something that engaged my children in books and reading.

There are atlas' for different ages, and there are other books of maps including maps of fantasy worlds, street directories (if you can find them, op shops and libraries may be the source of these), and travel guides.

Travel guides have maps as well as a lot of information about various places to visit.

Maps can be active when you follow them, such as a street directory, as well as be books you can pick up and put down with interest. They can also encourage the reader to research other areas and even plan a holiday or trip.

It can also be fun learning how to pronounce place names from countries you are unfamiliar with.

Conclusion

There are other types of books that may fall into 'active books' categories, and there is nothing to say that those with ADHD don't read novels, especially if they are novels they are interested in.

Reading doesn't have to be sitting still and reading a story, it can come in different forms.

For those with ADHD, a more active approach may be needed, as well as some creativity to find books based on interest.

Sometimes, getting engaged in reading simply takes a different approach. Try some of these strategies and have fun discovering some fantastic new books.

About the Author

Melissa Gijsbers is an author and booklover. Stories have always been a big part of her life and she has been writing them for as long as she can remember and reading for longer than that.

She was diagnosed with autism and ADHD in 2022 at the age of 44. She has been working with young writers since 2013 and combines her passion for stories with her knowledge and experience of being autistic and ADHD to help others fall in love with stories too.

She currently lives in Gippsland in Victoria, Australia and spends quite a bit of time coming up with fun writing ideas for stories, as well as writing more books herself.

You can find out more about Melissa and her books on her website—
www.melissagijsbers.com

Books by Melissa

- My Princess Wears a Superhero Cape
- My Mummy is Evil
- Swallow Me, NOW!
- 3… 2… 1… Done!
- Lizzy's Dragon
- Lilly's Library
- Genie in my Drink Bottle & other fun writing prompts
- Great Lost Sock Mystery & other writing prompts
- Writing Prompt Advent Calendar
- Writing Prompts – Random Words
- Creative Writing for Wellbeing

www.ingramcontent.com/pod-product-compliance
Lightning Source LLC
Chambersburg PA
CBHW071847290426
44109CB00017B/1961